First Facts®

Whales and Dolphins Up Close

KILLER WHALES Up CLOSE

by Jody Sullivan Rake

Consultant:
Deborah Nuzzolo
Education Manager
SeaWorld, San Diego

Capstone
press®

Mankato, Minnesota

First Facts is published by Capstone Press,
151 Good Counsel Drive, P.O. Box 669, Mankato, Minnesota 56002.
www.capstonepress.com

Library of Congress Cataloging-in-Publication Data
Rake, Jody Sullivan.
    Killer whales up close / by Jody Sullivan Rake.
    p. cm. — (First facts. Whales and dolphins up close)
    Includes bibliographical references and index.
    Summary: "Presents an up-close look at killer whales, including their body
features, habitat, and life cycle" — Provided by publisher.
    ISBN-13: 978-1-4296-2265-3 (hardcover)
    ISBN-10: 1-4296-2265-2 (hardcover)
    1. Killer whale — Juvenile literature. I. Title.
QL737.C432R356 2009
599.53'6 — dc22
                                                            2008030104

Editorial Credits
Christine Peterson, editor; Renée T. Doyle, designer; Wanda Winch, photo researcher

Photo Credits
Alamy/ImageState/Martin Ruegner, 18
iStockphoto/Evgeniya Lazareva, 11, 18 (inset)
Minden Pictures/Flip Nicklin, 12–13, 17; Hiroya Minakuchi, 15; Mark Carwardine, 21;
    Sue Flood, 20
Peter Arnold/BIOS Bios-Auteurs/Brandon Cole, 6–7; SplashdownDirect.com/Ingrid
    Visser, 5; SplashdownDirect.com/Michael Nolan, 7 (inset)
SeaPics.com/Ingrid Visser, 8; Jasmine Rossi, 16–17
Shutterstock, 24; Clarence S. Lewis, 1; David Pruter, 13 (inset), cover; Featherlightfoot,
    (blue spiral throughout); Timmary, (background throughout)

1 2 3 4 5 6 14 13 12 11 10 09

TABLE OF CONTENTS

Black and White and Awesome

Killer whales are fierce predators. Their giant bodies glide through cold ocean water. Their black-and-white skin feels like rubber. A thick layer of blubber keeps out the cold.

Killer whales are mammals. They breathe air and have warm bodies. Killer whales are also called orcas. They belong to the dolphin family. In fact, orcas are the world's largest dolphins.

Huge Hunters

Male killer whales are about the size of an elephant. They weigh 8,000 to 12,000 pounds (3,629 to 5,443 kilograms). Female killer whales are smaller.

All killer whales have long, triangular tail **flukes**. To swim, whales flip their strong tails up and down. The paddle-shaped flippers help them turn.

flipper

fluke — the wide, flat area at the end of a whale's tail

dorsal fin

Dorsal Fins

Sea animals know that a tall triangular shape means trouble. These triangles are **dorsal fins** on the backs of killer whales. You can easily spot adult males. Their dorsal fins can be 6 feet (1.8 meters) tall. Females have small, curved dorsal fins.

dorsal fin — a tall fin on a whale's back

blowhole

Blowholes

Like all mammals, killer whales need fresh air. Whales and dolphins use a **blowhole** on top of their heads to breathe. A strong flap covers the blowhole. The whale opens the flap to breathe out. Water over the blowhole shoots up in a cloud of spray. Underwater, the blowhole closes tightly.

blowhole — a hole on top of a whale's head

Worldwide Killer Whales

All the world's oceans are home to killer whales. Most swim in the icy Arctic and Antarctic. Killer whales can swim up to 30 miles (48 kilometers) per hour.

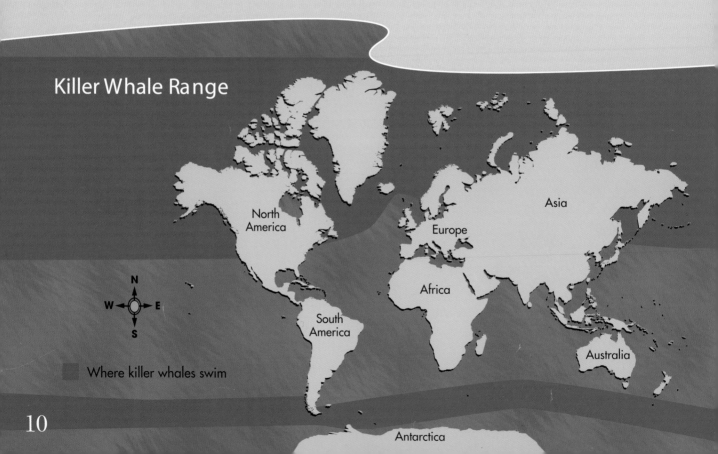

Killer Whale Range

North America

Europe

Asia

Africa

South America

Australia

N
W — E
S

Where killer whales swim

Antarctica

Killer whales live in groups called
pods. Most groups have from five to
30 killer whales. Killer whales in a group
are usually related.

pod — a group of whales

11

Communication

Killer whales talk to each other with calls. Their calls sound like a language. Different groups have their own calls. Young whales learn calls from the group.

Killer whales don't hear with just their ears. They hear most sounds through their lower jaw. The jaw acts like an antenna. It carries sounds to the inner ear and brain.

Killer Whale Life Cycle

Male and female killer whales mate to produce young. After 17 months, a female whale gives birth to a **calf**.

At birth, calves are about 8.5 feet (2.6 meters) in length. They weigh up to 400 pounds (181 kilograms). After one year, a calf doubles its size and is ready to hunt. Killer whales live about 30 to 35 years.

calf — a baby whale

Life Cycle of a Killer Whale

Calf
One killer whale calf is born at a time.

Mom and Baby

Young
In one year, young killer whales double in size.

Adult
Adult male and female killer whales mate to produce young.

15

Oceans of Food

Killer whales are the oceans' top **predator**. They feast on fish, seals, and otters. They even eat other whales and dolphins. Killer whales can eat 400 pounds (181 kilograms) of food a day.

Like wolves, killer whales often hunt together. They swim around prey and trap it. They also slide up on shore to snatch sea lions and penguins.

predator — an animal that hunts other animals for food

teeth

Terrific Teeth

Chomp! Killer whales grab prey with their sharp teeth. Their mouths are filled with 40 to 56 pointed teeth. Each tooth can be about 3 inches (7.6 centimeters) long. Their top and bottom teeth fit together like a zipper.

17

fluke

Jump, Dive, and Whale

Despite their huge size, killer whales have some amazing moves. They **breach**, or leap, out of the water. They splash down on their sides with a loud crash. They slap their tail flukes and flippers. Killer whales often **spyhop**. They poke their heads up to look around. They can also dive down 200 feet (61 meters).

breach — to jump out of the water
spyhop — when a whale pokes its head out of the water

Killer whales are fearless hunters. Just how fierce are they? Well, scientists have seen killer whales hunt gray whales and blue whales. Blue whales are the largest animals in the world. Killer whales have no predators. Not even sharks! If a great white shark attacked an adult killer whale, the shark would lose.

killer whale attacking a gray whale

Killer Whales and People

Some actions by people cause whale numbers to drop. When people catch too many fish, seals have fewer fish to eat. That means there are fewer seals for killer whales to eat. Water pollution also harms killer whales. People can enjoy and learn about killer whales in aquariums. The more people know, the better they can protect killer whales.

Glossary

blowhole (BLOH-hohl) — a hole on the top of a whale's head; whales breathe air through blowholes.

breach (BREECH) — to jump out of the water

calf (KAF) — a young whale, or dolphin

dorsal fin (DOR-suhl FIN) — the fin that sticks up from the middle of a whale's back

fluke (FLOOK) — the wide, flat area at the end of a whale's tail

pod (POD) — a group of whales

predator (PRED-uh-tur) — an animal that hunts other animals for food

spyhop (SPYE-hop) — a whale behavior in which it pokes its head out of the water

Read More

Adelman, Beth. *Killer Whales.* Boys Rock! Chanhassen, Minn.: Child's World, 2007.

Malam, John. *Killer Whales.* Scary Creatures. Danbury, Conn.: Franklin Watts, 2008.

Nicklin, Flip, and Linda Nicklin. *Face to Face with Whales.* Face to Face with Animals. Washington, D.C.: National Geographic, 2008.

Internet Sites

FactHound offers a safe, fun way to find educator-approved Internet sites related to this book.

Here's what you do:

1. Visit *www.facthound.com*
2. Choose your grade level.
3. Begin your search.

This book's ID number is 9781429622653.

FactHound will fetch the best sites for you!

Index